Summer Wine Country

Looking down the Holme Valley

CONTENTS

Cover photographs: (Top) Beautiful Summer Wine Countryside overlooking Digley Reservoir above Holmfirth; (Bottom Left) Howard and Marina enjoying a secret excursion into the hills and dales of Summer Wine Country; (Centre) Compo and Nora - will he ever win her heart? (Bottom Right) Clegg, Compo and Foggy up to their usual antics with this musical escapade.

Discovery Guides Limited wish to thank all those persons, organisations, official bodies and their officers, for their kind assistance in the production of this publication.

Photographs reproduced by kind permission of Malcolm Howarth unless indicated otherwise - those marked (K) are reproduced by courtesy of Kirklees Metropolitan Borough Council.

WRITTEN BY JOHN WATSON.   EDITED BY CAROLINE HILLERY.
SERIES EDITOR AND DESIGN MALCOLM PARKER.   ARTWORK AND DESIGN ANDREW FALLON.
PUBLISHED BY DISCOVERY PUBLISHING (UK) LTD.   PRINTED IN ENGLAND.
ISBN 0-86309-094-X   COPYRIGHT DISCOVERY PUBLISHING (UK) LTD.

D0256080

Introduction to the Area

Visitors to the Holme Valley in South Yorkshire often come to glimpse the locations of the hilarious exploits of their favourite characters from the long-running television series 'Last Of The Summer Wine'. Residents of Holmfirth are faced with a constant barrage of requests for directions to Sid's cafe, Nora Batty's house, and numerous other locations. Powerful as these characters are in the viewer's imagination, equally compelling is the **Summer Wine landscape** which forms such an enchanting scenic background to their antics.

THE NATURAL AGENTS which shape the landscape are the composition of surface rock strata, earth movements, glaciation, and constant weathering by wind, water and ice. Add to these man's **farming and industrial technology** throughout the ages, and we have the landscape we see today. As we survey our environment, we cannot fail to observe how just two momentous C20th aids to man's advancement, **the car and the aeroplane,** have scarred the countryside with a network of roads and a patchwork of airfields.

TELEVISION'S IMPACT on the social life of C20th man has been equally significant. But, unlike the car and aeroplane, it appears to have left the landscape relatively unscathed. Maybe the skyline has not been improved by a forest of sprouting aerials. On the other hand, the small number of television transmitter masts which taper skywards from some of Britain's highest hills, have even earned a kind of environmental respectability as useful landmarks. Indeed the boundaries of Summer Wine country are clearly marked out by three such transmitters towering over it: **Holme Moss** to the south, **Emley Moor** to the north-east and **Pole Moor** to the north-west.

A less obvious influence of television on the landscape has been the programmes themselves. Apart from acting as a general watchdog over potential countryside disfigurement, **television has turned to areas of outstanding natural beauty** as locations for light entertainment presentations. This is especially the case in Yorkshire with its dramatically photogenic scenery. The predominantly limestone scenery of the Yorkshire Dales has furnished the settings for two long-running television series **'All Creatures Great And Small'**, adapted from novels written by James Herriot and based on

his experiences as a vet in North Yorkshire; and the early episodes of the farming serial **'Emmerdale'**. In West Yorkshire, the millstone grit country of the South Pennines has created a natural backdrop for the equally popular **'Last Of The Summer Wine'** series, launched in 1972.

The charismatic quality of Summer Wine Country with its majestic hills, sweeping moors, verdant valleys, and narrow streets of grey stone villages must be visited and re-visited, not merely watched on television, if we are to capture the real essence of the region.

Compo beside a Pennine moorland stream

For many, the charm of Summer Wine Country and the delights of the small town of **Holmfirth** might have remained undiscovered, had they not been brought so vividly into their homes by this hugely popular situation comedy series. Not only does its action roam through the scenic splendours of Holmfirth and its surrounding countryside, but **Compo, Clegg and Co,** emerge as theatrical enlargements of actual people who have inhabited the **Holme Valley** for generations.

Ardent viewers of the TV series, engaging upon a serious or light-hearted pilgrimage to Summer Wine Country, cannot fail to come away with a more enlightened perception of the basic forces which have been at work in the creation of their favourite screen characters. Even the uninitiated viewer, on visiting the Holme Valley, will recognise how everywhere, over the centuries, man's activities have shaped the landscape and how in turn the landscape has shaped its people. Both are inextricably woven into that rich fabric which constitutes Summer Wine Country. Having tasted the **'bottled sunshine'** of this summer wine, the visitor should feel an irresistible urge to return and taste again.

The Rock of Ages

About 350 million years ago Summer Wine Country nestled beneath a tropical sea. The calcareous remains of sea-creatures compressed below its warm waters to form a **thick limestone bed** and, with time, massive earth movements trapped the sea. Rivers which rose in the north-eastern land mass drained into it, bringing with them mud, sand, and coarse grit. Under pressure, these deposits formed hard layers of rock, today called **Millstone Grit**, interspersed with softer limestone layers.

As the sea silted up, swamps engendered dense tropical vegetation. Constantly changing sea levels periodically buried this plant life. The **Carboniferous Period,** dating from about 300-230 million years ago, left as its legacy seams of coal inter-layered with sandstone, millstone, mudstone, limestone and shale strata. Then massive movements in the earth's crust began a period of folding, squeezing the deep-seated layers of rock and thrusting them upwards to form the north-south Pennine chain, a mountainous Millstone Grit formation flanked to east and west by isolated coal-fields.

About 2 million years ago began a series of about twelve **Ice Ages,** to continue the process of sculpting the Pennine chain into its present form. However, Summer Wine Country in the South Pennines was largely unaffected by the gouging and scouring action of these ice-sheets which receded about 12,000 years ago. When warmer conditions ensued, **glacial meltwaters** helped to feed streams and rivers of Summer Wine Country in their endless task of erosion, cutting out tributary cloughs and gorges, and broadening and deepening major valleys to east and west between steep gritstone escarpments.

Erosion, combined with the continual freeze-thaw process, has fashioned the craggy appearance of high-sided valleys, leaving rounded hill-tops and dramatic Millstone escarpments, like **Castle Hill,** etched into the skyline. Gritstone cap and fault-line waterfalls abound in Summer Wine Country. A particularly picturesque example near Meltham Mills is the **Folly Dolly Falls,** intriguingly named after a girl called Dorothy who killed herself in a leap from the cliff.

Poor Dolly's very early ancestors had arrived on the Summer Wine Country scene 10,000 years before her fatal leap. They emerged onto a landscape moulded by a frenzied geological past, but now cloaked in woodland. Initially early man found little comfort in the swamp-ridden valleys, and sought his survival on the high ground. **Woodland clearance** for settlement meant that tree-cover on the Summer Wine hills had disappeared by 2000 BC, thus aiding and abetting natural erosion. Without plant-life to absorb the minerals, rain washed them deep into the sub-soil to be compacted into a hard impermeable layer called the 'iron-pan', above which the moorland became waterlogged and acidic. Hence, **a build-up of peat** developed averaging 10 metres (30 feet) in depth.

Looking across Digley Reservoir

Geological forces had created in Summer Wine Country a sumptuous storehouse to be exploited down the corridors of time by man for his social and economic needs. Initially a rich topsoil had fostered the growth of vegetation, providing wood and peat for building, as well as sources of heat and light. Sheep could thrive in an ideal environment. The fast-flowing streams of the precipitous narrow valleys served as a source of power for early corn-mills, and the later textile mills, while the softness of the water was ideal for a thriving **woollen industry.** Tough millstone grit ensured an adequate supply of grindstones, without which the **Sheffield cutlery industry** could not have flourished. There were plenteous supplies of **building stone.**

Today the landscape of Summer Wine Country everywhere bears the distinctive imprint of man down the ages, who in his comparatively short lifetime, has sought to fashion the building-blocks of millions of years of geological turbulence to his essential survival needs.

The Passage of Time

Although early man had begun to tame the Summer Wine landscape and had denuded the hill-tops of trees, the inhospitable climate and terrain tested even the resolute entrepreneurial spirit of the **Roman invaders** of the C1st AD. They gave it a miss, preferring to open up essential cross-Pennine routes on the periphery of Summer Wine Country. In so doing, the **Romans** provided access to Summer Wine Country for successive invaders of **Angles, Saxons** and **Norsemen**. These 'comers-in' continued the rapacious enterprise of deforestation further down the hillsides, shaping the landscape to embrace their agricultural technology and animal husbandry. The **Vikings** particularly have left a rich legacy of their language in present-day place-names and landscape features of Summer Wine Country.

In 1066 the **Normans** found the countryside ideal for establishing their beloved hunting forests. They brought organisation to community farming methods. Fairs and markets in expanding hamlets began to provide outlets for produce. Under the manorial and parish systems, woodland clearance was extended down into the valleys and water harnessed in the service of corn-mills.

Agriculture was limited by the topography, climate and mineral-leached soils. By the C13th farming incomes had to be supplemented by a **cottage weaving industry**, so creating a dual economy. As the demand for cloth to satisfy more than local needs expanded, hillside hamlets could no longer cope. Thus, cottage weavers were attracted to form **riverside settlements** in the drained valleys, water-driven fulling-mills being established alongside corn-mills. Local trade routes expanded further afield. Many of the present-day Summer Wine Country lanes and roads were carved out by **pack-horse trains**, laden with exported textile goods on outward journeys, to return with imported products and raw materials essential to a burgeoning Summer Wine economy.

By the C16th, the increasing wealth of yeoman farmers and clothiers induced them to replace their timber houses in stone, a trend soon followed by many lower down the social scale. **The domestic handloom weavers created an enduring style of architecture.** Standing proudly on Summer Wine hillsides are their two or three-storey cottages, with long rows of mullioned windows on the upper floors to light the looms inside. The development of stone villages continued throughout the C17th and C18th, where today they form a haphazard and arresting picture perched precipitously on the hillsides.

The pretty Folly Dolly Falls

The C18th and C19th market, greedy for cloth, could only be satisfied by speeding up the textile processes. The lightning transformation of weaving from a cottage industry to a water-driven, and then to a coal-powered mill industry, began with the introduction of the 'flying shuttle' in 1733. The 'spinning jenny', the 'mule', water-wheel and steam-engines all followed in quick succession. **The Industrial Revolution** completely transformed the Summer Wine landscape, its sylvan valleys tightly packed with mill chimneys belching smoke, its hillsides scarred with gaping quarries and crammed with terraced cottages overloaded with a hungry and exploited work force. Amidst this grotesque mushroom growth stood **buildings conceived on the grand scale;** mansions of mill-owners, flamboyant town halls, solid chapels and churches, ornate churchyard mausoleums, all reflecting a civic pride in hard-won industrial prosperity.

The industrial expansion of the Summer Wine economy mirrored the overall development in national importance of the South Pennine textile industry. C17th packhorse routes were an inadequate means of transport and gave way to roads constructed under the supervision of Turnpike Trusts. **'Turnpike mania'** became an C18th national epidemic. Under the influence of pioneer road-builders, turnpike roads were soon snaking their way across Summer Wine Country.

At the onset of the C19th road-building engineering feats were eclipsed by a new epidemic, this time **'canal mania'**. The **Huddersfield Narrow Canal** in the Colne Valley on the southern boundary of Summer Wine Country remains supreme in canal engineering history, not only having the distinction of being the highest canal in Great Britain, but in possessing **Standedge Tunnel**, the longest canal tunnel in the land.

John Watson, the author, at Eastergate Bridge

The life of canals was comparatively short-lived, as C19th **'railway mania'** took hold alongside accelerated industrial development. **A branch line from Huddersfield to Holmfirth** in 1850 penetrated into the heartland of the Holme Valley. The southern boundary of Summer Wine Country saw the construction of the **Standedge Railway Tunnel**, running parallel to the canal tunnel. Meanwhile, the northern boundary was fringed by the **Woodhead Tunnel**, in 1845 the longest in Britain, forming a link in the trans-Pennine Manchester-Sheffield railway.

Summer Wine Country was a savage beast to tame, however, and man had to pay a high price for his hard-won success. The constant uphill battle against a rugged terrain and an inhospitable climate has taken a heavy toll in lives. Famine and plagues were an ever-present threat to early development. Behind the facade of well-being engendered by the Industrial Revolution lurked the dark satanic image of appalling working conditions, a smoke-polluted atmosphere, the exploitation of child labour, cramped housing, poor sanitation and consequent outbreaks of cholera. Deprivation led to acts of vandalism against machinery, and then discontent vented against the pernicious **Poor Law** in the 1830s. Trying to find solace in non-conformist religion was only achieved after a long and bitter struggle. Even water, a major contributor to the Summer Wine success story, from time to time has turned its creative force to devastatingly destructive ends. Flash flooding in 1738, 1777, 1944, and the burst dam of **Bilberry Reservoir** which caused the **Great Flood of 1852**, all transformed the River Holme into a raging torrent, pursuing a remorseless downhill course, and leaving in its wake a trail of death and destruction through the Holme Valley.

For 10,000 years man had struggled to harness Summer Wine Country to his survival needs. By the beginning of the C20th the beast was tamed, and fully yoked in the service of cloth. But the battle was not over. When the First World War began in 1914, the zenith of prosperity had been reached. **After the War in 1918, the textile industry began its decline** in face of overseas competition. Out-dated machinery in cramped valley conditions and a lack of investment, both meant that Summer Wine Country was not in a position to incorporate new automated industrial processes required to compete in world markets. The steady pace of decline became a gallop after 1945.

But 10,000 years of struggle with Summer Wine Country had not been in vain. Adversity had strengthened man's indomitable spirit. **Phoenix-like, a regenerative process which began in the 1950s is still gaining momentum today.** Clearing away the ugly and cumbersome detritus of a largely redundant industrial past has been paralleled by a programme of conservation of all that is worth preserving of its former glories. Adaptation, diversification and the introduction of **new forms of employment** have been encouraged, with the retail economy and tourism being high on the list. Local Authorities, Government Agencies, private businesses and voluntary sectors of the community have all combined to revitalize the environment, economy and lifestyle of an area which historically has proved itself capable of survival. The scene is set for the next act in this long-running drama to be played out upon the Summer Wine stage.

An Earlier Era of Film Stardom

Today the Holme Valley owes much of its wide public appeal to television exposure in the **'Last of the Summer Wine'** series. However, producers of this series were not the first to recognise the screen potential of its captivating landscape. In the early C19th **Bamforth and Co. of Holmfirth** were on course for establishing Summer Wine Country as the centre of the world's motion picture industry, long before Hollywood came into existence.

JAMES BAMFORTH, a postcard printer since 1870, was among the earliest film-making pioneers. As an artist, he utilised Holme Valley vistas as painted backdrops to live models of local people, who became the early screen 'stars' of thousands of lantern slides which were put together in sequence. From 1899 onwards, **short silent movies**, in the style of later Hollywood Max Sennet films, enthralled local audiences in depicting popular songs and stories of the day. **Films began to be shot in realistic local settings.** Holme Valley businesses lent their support, with banks opening their doors for fake bank raids, the railway company providing special trains, and the Holmfirth Council allowing use of the park. From these early comedies developed adventure, romance, and crime films. **Demand escalated and offices were opened in London and New York.** Then, an order for 100 films made for Russia was abruptly halted with the outbreak of war in 1914. This was the end of Holmfirth's journey towards international film stardom. After the war, it was decided that further development in filming was impracticable because of the lack of sunlight in the area.

Besides, the 1914-18 War had opened up new opportunities for Bamforths. As men left to fight in foreign fields, a large demand was rekindled for heart-breaking **sentimental greetings-cards**, first printed by Bamforths during the Boer War. Pretty local girls, previously in films, were now transferred to postcards depicting lovers saying 'Goodbye', and illustrating verses of such sentimental songs as 'Goodbye Dolly Gray'.

AFTER THE WAR, laughter was quick to replace dewy-eyed sentiment on the emotional scene, and Bamforth's were on hand to exploit a new vogue - **saucy seaside postcards,** so much part of the holiday tradition which the British enjoy. The company's present-day fame is reflected in these postcards with their titillatingly 'rude' captions. Red-faced drunks, weedy hen-pecked husbands, busty females of the alluring and termagant varieties, cheeky kids, all became the new postcard heroes. Do you recognise any of the 'Last Of The Summer Wine' characters amongst these Bamforth caricatures?

BAMFORTH AND CO, still producing saucy seaside postcards alongside those of scenic views, is housed in Station Road, Holmfirth. The large expanse of windows in the premises echoes the rows of mullioned windows on the old weavers' cottages, so allowing the maximum entry of light to aid the work of designers and cartoonists. Bamforth's illustrious past is brought to life in the impressive **Holmfirth Postcard Museum** where the visitor is not only certain of a good laugh, but can trace how humour has changed over the last century, as well as gaining an insight into early movie-making. A stick of Holmfirth rock can be taken home, or visitors can become part of the Bamforth tradition by being photographed with their heads through the family seaside scene!

'At the seaside' published by Bamforth & Co

The promenade emporiums of British seaside resorts provide in their 'mucky' postcards a jocular reminder of the **continuing fame of Bamforth's of Holmfirth.** However, but for the 1914-18 War, the early fame of Bamforths as movie-makers might have transformed the landscape of the Holme Valley into another Hollywood, its hillsides stripped of their industrial past in favour of Beverley Hills-style mansions and swimming pools! Nevertheless, 'The Last Of The Summer Wine' series, and today's frequent presence of film crews and actors on the natural sets of Summer Wine villages and countryside, evoke memories of Bamforth's glorious cinematic past. They confirm that **the Summer Wine landscape has not lost its power to bewitch** today's film moguls.

'Summer Wine' Humour

Burnlee Working Men's Club in the early 1970s was situated close to Holmfirth. At that time it was presenting a form of entertainment which had become associated with many industrial areas of Britain - crude humour, raunchy songs and titillating striptease. **TV presenter Barry Took** was assigned to use Burnlee WMC as a springboard to an appraisal of Holmfirth and district. The programme was entitled **'Having A Lovely Time'**, thus echoing a greeting so familiar on Bamforth's saucy seaside postcards. Press reviews did not flatter the programme, the Daily Mirror commenting that Took's view of the region was 'lifeless, cheerless and dejected'.

Fortunately a writer, **Roy Clarke**, and a BBC TV director, **James Gilbert**, saw in the captivating Holme Valley landscape and its down-to-earth, real-life characters an idea for a TV situation comedy series. It was from this idea that **'Last Of The Summer Wine'**, was born. A pilot TV episode was launched in 1971 and a BBC commission followed in 1972. So popular has the series proved to be that it is still flourishing today.

Though Holmfirth is never identified by name in the series, under the influence of 'Last of the Summer Wine' its surrounding area has became more familiarly known as **'Summer Wine Country'**. In fact, part of the success of the series is attributable to the landscape locations which serve as backdrops to the antics of its characters. The visual attraction of Summer Wine Country is summed up by a Last of the Summer Wine cameraman, **Alan Stevens**: 'The nature's here, the beauty's here, it's a beautiful part of the world'. **Juliette Kaplan**, who plays the part of Pearl, confirms this view in recording a southerner's first impression of a countryside she had been led to believe was drab and smoky: '...shades of green and gold, crystal lakes (I don't care if they are reservoirs!), rising hills of such beauty that I felt I was in a different world'. **Sarah Thomas**, Glenda in the series, is equally fulsome in her praise of the landscape: 'When the sun comes out over Summer Wine hills, it's just magical'.

THE SUMMER WINE LOCATIONS are all the more fascinating in that they encapsulate the area's industrial history. Age-old mills, dams, reservoirs, canals, farmsteads, packhorse bridges, quarries, chapels, pubs, dry-stone walls, weavers' cottages, mill-workers' terraced houses, cobblestone sets, steps and narrow ginnels, all provide settings which combine to satisfy the viewers' search for their historic past. Summer Wine Country has preserved so much of its heritage that it is an **ideal playground for geriatric characters** who are re-living their more youthful days. Though the action of 'Last of the Summer Wine' takes place in the present, the flavour of the series evokes nostalgic memories of days gone by. An experimental by-product of Last of the Summer Wine, **'First Of The Summer Wine'**, took the viewer back in time, and Summer Wine Country was perfect for this transformation. 'In Holmfirth and Upperthong you just have to scratch away the dust and you have the 1930s' was how Alan Stevens put it.

Compo, Seymour & Clegg playing Santa

THE CHARACTERS in 'Last of the Summer Wine' are as engaging as their settings. They too have a flavour of yesteryear. Their creator, Roy Clarke, has given them personality traits and attitudes which were etched into their real-life counterparts in their struggle to survive down the ages. Hardship and insecurity sharpens wit and shapes humour in defiance of unfulfilled hopes and dreams, and as a cushion against despair. A sense of humour is essential to survival, and it is this humour which pervades **Roy Clarke's** Last of the Summer Wine characters, **Compo, Clegg, Foggy Dewhurst, Seymour Utterthwaite**, and Blamires from an early episode, all cling to dreams of what they might have been. In Compo, the archetypal sponger and layabout, lies a strong Yorkshire non-conformist streak -

Bill Owen, who plays Compo, describes him as 'a geriatric Just William'. All of these characters are in the twilight of their years, but stoically refuse to give in. They live out their days revelling in second childhood, rebelliously defying old age. We laugh at them because in them we see our own hopes and fears and admire their defiance.

In **Nora Batty, Ivy, Edie, Pearl** and **Auntie Wainwright** lie the sharp-tongued termagant women so typically illustrated on Bamforth's saucy seaside postcards. The hen-pecked 'Last of the Summer Wine' men stand no chance in the battle of the sexes. They are defeated at every turn by women who are in closer touch with reality than their menfolk, and at a glance can see through male strategies when 'they're up to something'. These female creations hark back to the days when it was indisputable that a woman's place was in the home. Amongst their daily household tasks lay responsibility for curbing the fanciful escapades of their chauvinistic menfolk, when they threatened to endanger the well-being of family life. **Nora Batty** sums up the situation in one of her lines from the series: 'Men must be well-trained. You can do practically anything with them, provided you keep them away from their own kind.' Not to be defeated by such a perceptive female comment, Compo's riposte might be: 'If Nora Batty had driven a chariot, you wouldn't have been able to see the fleeing Romans for dust', said of course at a coward's distance beyond Nora's hearing! This battle for sexual domination is the source of much of the humour of Last of the Summer Wine. It is entertainingly depicted in the endless hamfisted attempts of a lewd Compo to win the unattainable affections of Nora Batty, who defends her honour with a broom, or in the efforts of a browbeaten Howard to deceive his hectoring wife, Pearl, over his clandestine affair with Marina, the ageing femme fatale.

ROY CLARKE'S WORLD is peopled by characters holding on to traditional values handed down by their real-life predecessors. We are recalled to a time when 'brass' was short, when it was the fashion to '**mek summat out of nowt**', when 'makking game' of grim circumstances was the order of the day. It produced a people with plain but proud tastes, resistant to the opinions of others, suspicious of the outside world, and hostile to change. Such attitudes are reflected in the unchanging nature of the characters' clothing - Nora Batty's wrinkled stockings, Compo's wellies, Wesley's overalls, floral print frocks, bloomers, pinafores, cloche hats, curlers, stout and sober coats, and suits, cloth-caps, long johns, all

speak of a former age when habit was an unquestioned virtue. Breaking of routine demanded comment. When Compo is offered sherry instead of the customary sacred glass of beer he is appalled: 'Sherry? I wouldn't varnish me ferret with that stuff!' Then, spying Nora Batty, he says: 'Nora Batty dressed up on a Wednesday? She must be going the doctor's.' Nora Batty is horrified when she espies a couple, married for 50 years, still holding hands in the street: 'It's a bit excessive! Too continental for my taste. I'm not sure I approve of holding hands in the street!' Definitely not '**Yorkshire Respectable!**'

HABIT AND CUSTOM LIVE ON in Roy Clarke's 'Last of the Summer Wine' characters. We laugh at their obstinate refusal to change, but within our laughter lies an approval of their single-minded determination to remain as they are. They also tap in us the nostalgic hankering after '**the good old days**', even if closer examination reveals them to be 'the bad old days'. It was in these 'bad old days' that this unique brand of humour and genius for picturesque self-expression was formed within the Summer Wine people. In his book, 'Summer Wine Country', Roy Clarke writes a letter in the name of the 'Last of the Summer Wine' character Norman Clegg. In it he speaks about Summer Wine people: 'We are a hill people... Up and down is our way of life. Gravity has a reality hereabouts..'.. Out of this gravity comes humour. As Bill Owen says, '**Comedy is a serious business.**'

Compo, Nora Batty and a touch of romance

'Summer Wine' in the Making

Did you know that 'Last of the Summer Wine' is the longest running and most expensive comedy series made by the BBC? - that it would take nearly **60 hours of continuous viewing** to see over **100 episodes and 4 full length films?** - that the Christmas episode 'Whoops' shown in 1981 rated 18 million viewers, whereas 'Gone With The Wind', screened over the same period, rated only 14 million?

THESE INTRIGUING FACTS, and many others, can be gleaned at the **'Last Of The Summer Wine Exhibition'** housed in Holmfirth. It is an absorbing Aladdin's Cave of 'Last of the Summer Wine' photographs and memorabilia. Its custodian, Malcolm Howarth, is on hand with all you need to know about this popular TV series. From here it is a short car journey to Jackson Bridge and **The White Horse Inn,** whose exterior is the location for many 'Last of the Summer Wine' episodes. The bar interior has been reproduced in detail in the studio to serve as the local 'Last of the Summer Wine' watering-hole, though occasionally it has been used for location shots when rain has curtailed outside filming. Photographs bedeck the walls and almost provide an entire history of 'Last of the Summer Wine'. Where there are omissions, mine host, Ron Backhouse, has a fund of stories to tell about the filming of 'Last of the Summer Wine' over the years.

THE SUMMER WINE LANDSCAPE is so rich in photographic potential that it is hard to find a corner which has not functioned as a 'Last of the Summer Wine' location. At its heart, **Holmfirth** must have become the most filmed small town ever to appear on television screens. Thousands of visitors on a 'Last of the Summer Wine' pilgrimage are drawn each year to Sid's cafe in the paved area near the church. Next in line, nestled alongside the picturesque River Holme in Hollowgate, are **the homes of Compo and Nora,** which are private dwellings and not open to the public. Hardly an episode goes by when the exteriors of these two 'Last of the Summer Wine' shrines do not feature. Their interiors too have been used for filming, but because of their restricted space and inconvenience to owners, most interior scenes are shot in London studio settings.

It is one of the jobs of the Production Manager to search out **exterior locations,** which range from churchyards to scrapyards! Even if the Producer/Director finds a selected location scenically appropriate, negotiations must then take place with owners of buildings or land. A location can be ruled out because of a lack of parking-space for up to 35 vehicles, which include cars; generator; lighting, props, visual effects and caterers' wagons; costume and make-up caravan; sound effects estate car; bus to transport actors and film crew; and of course toilets housed in what is known as 'the honeywagon'! The police must be consulted and their help enlisted for such a vast cavalcade to negotiate the narrow country roads and village streets. On town and village locations crowds of curious well-wishers have to be catered for, as they clamour for photographs and autographs amidst actors, film cameras and crews, dazzling arc lights, microphones, and electric cables littering the pavements. To ease pressure on local inhabitants going about their daily business, the 8 weeks filming on location for a 10 half-hour series is spread over separate fortnightly 'takes'.

Filming in a moorland location

Locations are often used in Marsden in the Colne Valley to lessen the strain on Holmfirth and district. The 'Last of the Summer Wine' team are unanimous in their praise of the patience and co-operation of local people, when their peace is shattered by traffic jams and parking becomes a nightmare.

Hillside locations also provide their problems, particularly the unpredictable weather. Cows and sheep remain undisturbed by the familiar sight of actors at 7.30am going over their lines as they wait for the action to begin, warding off the rigours of dank, misty mornings with thick jumpers, wellies, thermal underwear, and fortifying mugs of tea and bacon butties. Hopefully, a sub-gale force wind will clear the fog to reveal a Summer Wine Country in all its sunlit glory before filming ends, sometimes at 7.00pm. If not, then the arc lights are there to substitute for a reluctant sun and recreate the balmy days of yore! Of course, the bright day, so cherished by all film-makers, can be the very day when rain is required for a scene! Then out comes a rain-machine. What more incongruous sight can there be than a rain-machine in Summer Wine Country?

STUNTS HAVE TO BE ARRANGED and stuntmen engaged to satisfy the 'Last of the Summer Wine' demand for broad humour. The precipitous Summer Wine hillsides provide ideal locations for **Seymour Utterthwaite's zany inventions** to run out of control, carrying their intrepid heroes with them. Canals, dams and streams are there for their comic potential to be exploited. The actors cope with the milder stunts themselves, but trained stuntmen take on the more dangerous feats. Actors are too valuable a commodity to have them risk injury. After all, such is the agility of the actors playing those three hair-brained rascals, that it is easy to forget that their combined age is in excess of 200 years!

Once location and studio filming is completed, the lengthy process of cutting and editing takes place and the music of Ronny Hazelhurst is added. Then each episode of a series is unveiled on monitor before a studio audience. Their laughter is superimposed on the soundtrack as the filmed action unfolds, thus avoiding 'canned' laughter and contributing to the spontaneity of the programme. All is ready for transmission.

Last of the Summer Wine's author, Roy Clarke, achieved success with another TV situation comedy series, 'Open All Hours'. But it is a remarkably sustained feat to have scripted every episode of the 'Last of the Summer Wine' series over its lengthy run,

during which time it has earned, amongst many accolades, the Pye Colour Television Award for the best-written TV comedy. Roy Clarke has been admirably served by the producer/directors of the series: **James Gilbert** in 1971-2; then **Sydney Lotterby,** fresh from producing '**Yes, Minister**' and from 1981 to the present day, **Alan Bell,** who directed the full-length TV films of the series. All of them have had the long-standing backing of a regiment of production staff and camera crews.

SUCH A GALAXY OF STARS have been brought to our screens in 'Last of the Summer Wine' that to chronicle them all, together with their stage and screen successes, would demand a publication of mammoth proportions. To attempt such a task would run the risk of omissions, unforgivable with a cast which prides itself on working as a team. It must suffice to record that **still with the series since 1971 are: Bill Owen as Compo; Peter Sallis as Clegg; Kathy Staff as Nora Batty; and Jane Freeman as Ivy.** It is a tribute to their love of the series that they have stayed so long. Of course, over such a long-running series 'Last of the Summer Wine' has known its share of sadness with the deaths of: **Michael Bates** - Blamire; **John Comer** - Sid, the cafe owner and husband of Ivy; and **Joe Gladwin** - Nora Batty's husband, Wally.

'Last of the Summer Wine' actors and technical staff, past and present, have no doubt about their affections for the series, for Summer Wine Country and its people. **The words of Bill Owen not long ago seem to echo so many of their feelings:** 'Eighteen years of watching the face of Holmfirth change, but secure in the knowledge that its folk have remained the same - warm, friendly Tykes, who have taken me in and made me feel one of them. Eighteen years. It has become a way of life for me. Holmfirth is home. London is the place I have to live in.'

Compo, Clegg & Seymour at Seymour's workshop

A Holmfirth Town Trail

1. **This 2.5 mile (4 km) trail begins between the Information Centre and The Library on Huddersfield Road.**

2. Behind them lies **Victoria Park,** an area of land bought partly by public subscription in 1897 to commemorate Queen Victoria's Diamond Jubilee. In 1906 it was given to the local Council. At its centre is the reconstructed C18th doorway of **Yateholme Farm,** once situated near the village of Holme and recorded in the Domesday Book in 1086. The doorway was moved to this site when Batley Corporation demolished Yateholme Farm to construct its reservoirs. It is in Victoria Park that the **Holmfirth Sing** has been held annually before Whitsuntide, since 1882, to celebrate Holmfirth Feast.

3. **Holmfirth Postcard Museum** houses a collection of 30,000 comic postcards created over the past 100 years by **Bamforths,** whose pioneering work in the motion picture industry is recorded in a video of silent films. Another video details the dramatic events surrounding **the Holmfirth Flood of 1852.**

Nora Batty's House in Holmfirth (K)

4. The studio of **Ashley Jackson** is home to this internationally famed water-colour artist whose landscape paintings vividly portray Summer Wine Country.

5. Only about 300 yards from the centre of Holmfirth is the idyllic setting of **Prickleden Dam,** which has served as a location for the watery exploits of the intrepid heroes of the 'Last of the Summer Wine' series.

6. **The Toll House Book Shop** is on the site of the Toll Bar, which served the early C19th Huddersfield to Woodhead and Enterclough Bridge Turnpike Road. The original Toll Bar House was swept away in the Holmfirth Flood of 1852. Standing opposite, from 1706 until it was demolished in 1969, was the **King's Head Tavern,** known locally as The White Door.

7. Alongside the river is **Scarfold,** private dwellings which serve as homes to Compo and Nora Batty in the 'Last of the Summer Wine' series. Whilst this location evokes vivid memories of the series, it is interesting to ponder how the fig trees below these houses found such an unlikely location as the banks of the River Holme!

8. **The Elephant and Castle** is a former coaching inn, situated where the Turnpike Road crossed the river. An inn of the same

name was there before 1822. Note the brass plate left of the door which draws attention to the height of the 1944 flood.

9. A quaint lane called **Goose Green** which for hundreds of years was a busy thoroughfare to south-east hillside hamlets. A goose fair was possibly held on this site.

10. **Hollowgate** became the original **Turnpike Road.** Before this, the fields which flanked it and the river housed the first fair in 1725 and **the first Holmfirth Feast in 1726.**

11. Originally known as **The Nook**, now called **Back o't'Nook**, it crosses the ancient **Higgin Brig** which was the main road through Holmfirth before the Turnpike Road. The present-named pub, **The Nook**, was formerly The Rose and Crown.

12. **A Cafe**, once a fish and chip shop, features as Sid's and Ivy's cafe in the 'Last of the Summer Wine' series.

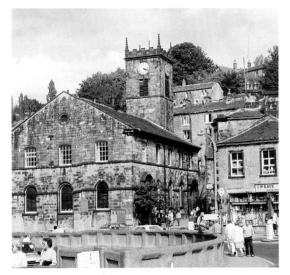

Holmfirth Town Centre

13. **The Church of the Holy Trinity** is on the site of perhaps an early wooden church, and certainly the first stone church built in 1476. This was replaced in 1632 by a large building for a congregation of 600. In 1651 the Chapelry of Holmfirth became a separate parish until the restoration of Charles II, when it reverted to a Chapel-of-Ease in the Parish of Kirkburton. Holmfirth did not become a fully independent parish until 1858. Meanwhile, flood damage to the Church in 1777 resulted in the present Georgian Church replacing it, with its tower and six bells added in 1788. In 1688 the church had gained notoriety when the vicar, the **Reverend Edmund Robinson**, was hanged at York for supplementing his

stipend by indulging in the unlawful practice of 'clipping and coining'.

14. Opposite the Church is a building which in 1912 was the **Holme Valley Theatre**, one of the earliest Picture Houses in the country.

Sid and Ivy's Cafe in Holmfirth

15. Up the steps behind the Church is a small squat building, known locally as **Th'owd Towser**, a name derived from the one-time village constables, Owd Dontley and Dransfield. It is **thought to be the oldest building in Holmfirth, dating back to 1597** when it was a church lock-up. Empty now, from time to time it has functioned as a mortuary, jail, ambulance and fire station.

16. Up another flight of steps, and in a wall on the right about 30 metres up the slope of Bunkers Hill, are two circular indentations which are **'wuzzing' holes**. In these holes a rod was lodged and a basket containing wet wool was wuzzed around it, acting as an C18th spin-drier used by cottage weavers.

17. The upper block of houses beyond the wuzzing holes is known as **Rattle Row**, named as a result of the rattle of handlooms once housed there.

18. Situated in Towngate is **Th'owd Genn**, possibly named after a local Wooldale sculptor, **Henry Genn**. It commemorates the

short **Peace of Amiens** which was signed in 1802, though strangely the memorial bears the date 1801! The Peace of Amiens brought a temporary halt to the war which had broken out with France in 1793. At first the war had meant an increased demand for cloth for uniforms from Holmfirth clothiers, a short-lived boost which was offset by a sharp decrease in overseas trade. Holmfirth rejoiced in the Peace of Amiens which heralded a restoration of valuable overseas markets for cloth. The Th'owd Genn also bears a plate recording the height of the 1852 flood water.

19. **At the end of Towngate** on the left, it is worth looking into the gardens. The flagged path of gravestones testifies to a former graveyard site.

The popular folk festival in Holmfirth (K)

20. **On the right of Station Road is a building housing Bamforths,** the firm established by James Bamforth in 1870 which was to gain an international reputation for pioneering motion pictures, and later for its production of sentimental and saucy seaside postcards. For over 100 years the large expanse of windows on the first floor have let in the light needed to aid Bamforth's army of artists and illustrators.

21. Uphill, 100 metres from Bamforths, is the impressive Regency frontage of the **Druids' Hall** built in the mid-C19th by The Order of Druids Friendly Society. In its time it has served as a meeting-place for Free Methodists and later for early Socialists, as well as a Drill Hall and Entertainments Hall. Today it is the home of the Masonic Lodge.

22. Further uphill on Station Road are a group of **five Gothic-style almshouses,** originally topped by an elegant spire which has since been removed. These were built by public subscription to house victims of the 1852 Holmfirth Flood.

23. Descending Station Road are seen the remains of **the old Railway Station**, the terminus of the Lancashire and Yorkshire Railway Company branch line from Huddersfield, built in 1850. The passenger service ceased in 1959 and goods services in 1965.

24. Passing through the Station yard and crossing the river, **the building on the right in Bridge Lane was the Police Station,** constructed in 1857 to house a police inspector and three prison cells. It is now part of an adjoining building, the **Institute of Adult Education,** erected in 1894 as **Holmfirth Technical College,** to provide courses 'for the diffusion and advancement of education, thrift and industry, science, literature and art'.

25. Turning left onto Huddersfield Road, is **the Civic Hall.** This two-storey building is constructed of square blocks of hewn stone, a style known as 'ashlar'. In effect it is two adjoining buildings combined, one being the **old Town Hall** built in 1842 for £2,200 raised in shares, the other formerly being **the Drill Hall** opened in 1892 to house the Holmfirth Volunteers who previously had been drilled in the Druids' Hall.

26. **The Methodist Chapel Schoolroom,** whose exterior has featured as the library in the 'Last of the Summer Wine' series. Behind it is the modern **Methodist Chapel** which recently replaced the 1871 building, which in turn had superseded the original 1787 chapel.

27. **The Post Office and car park** stand on a site previously occupied by the water-driven **Holmfirth Mill,** where it is presumed a corn mill has been sited ever since the very early Soke Mill, owned by the Earls of Warren in Edward II's reign.

28. It is fitting that this Town Trail ends at the **'Last Of The Summer Wine' Exhibition** on Huddersfield Road. It is here that 19 years of 'Last of the Summer Wine' history can be traced in photographs and memorabilia, a history which has lured so many visitors to Holmfirth and Summer Wine Country to delve into its fascinating past.

General Map of the Area

KEY

ℹ	Tourist Information
☀	Viewpoint
🏛	Art Gallery/Museum
	Land above 500 metres (1500ft approx)
	Land above 250 metres (800ft approx)
	Land below 250 metres (800ft approx)
	Lakes/Reservoirs

M62
A672
A640
M62
B6114
A640

Buckstones Moss 463m

Scapegoat Hill
Colne Valley Museum
River Colne
A62
Pole Moor
Golcar
Slaithwaite
Linthwaite

Hey Green
Tunnel End Canal & Countryside Centre
Deer Hill Reservoir
Blackmoorfoot Reservoir
B6108
Hon

Standedge
A62
Tunnel
Marsden
B6107
Meltham
Neth

West Nab 500m
Wessenden Reservoir
N
Holmfirth Postcard Mus
Upperthong

0   5 kms
Approximate Scale
0   3 Miles

A635
Austonley
Last Sumn Exhi
Digley Reservoir
Holmbri
Brownhill Reservoir
Holme
Had

Black Hill 582m
HOLME MOSS
COOK'S STUDY

A6024
The Pennine Way
Woodhead Tunne

Holmfirth Town Trail
(Approx. 3½ miles - 6kms)

1. Tourist Information
2. Victoria Park
3. Holmfirth Postcard Museum
4. Ashley Jackson's Studio
5. Prickleden Dam
6. Toll House Bookshop
7. Scarfold
8. The Elephant and Castle
9. Goose Green
10. Hollowgate
11. Back o't'Nook
12. Cafe
13. Holy Trinity Church
14. Holme Valley Theatre
15. Th'owd Towser
16. Wuzzing Holes
17. Rattle Row
18. Th'owd Genn
19. Gardens
20. Bamforth's
21. Druids Hall
22. Almshouses
23. Railway Station
24. Institute of Adult Education
25. Civic Hall
26. Methodist Chapel and Schoolroom
27. Post Office and Car Park
28. Last of the Summer Wine Exhibition

0   Kilometres   3
Approximate Scale

Wood Lane
Hightown Lane
Huddersfield Road
Bridge Lane
Station Road
Wood Lane
Carr House Road
Cooper Lane
A6024
School St
Back Lane
Station Road
Towngate
Binns Lane
Upperthong Lane
Little Lane
A635 Greenfield Road
Woodhead Road
River Holme
New Fold
Victoria Street
Hollowgate
Rotcher Road
Back o't Nook
South Lane
B6106 Dunford Road
Goose Green

Victoria Park
START + FINISH
N

TOURIST INFORMATION CENTRES

NORTH WEST TOURIST BOARD
Swan House, Swan Meadow Road,
Wigan Pier, Wigan,
Lancashire, WN3 5BB
Tel: (01942) 821222

BARNSLEY
56 Eldon Street, Barnsley,
South Yorkshire, S70 2JL
Tel: (01226) 206757

BRADFORD
c/o National Museum of
Photography, Film & Television,
Pictureville, Bradford, BD1 1NQ
Tel: (01274) 753678

BURNLEY
Burnley Mechanic
Manchester Road
Lancashire, BB11
Tel: (01282) 455-

GLOSSOP
The Gatehouse,
Victoria Street, Gl
Derbyshire, SK13
Tel: (01457) 855

HALIFAX
The Piece Hall, H,
West Yorkshire, H
Tel: (01422) 368

HAWORTH
2-4 West Lane, H.
West Yorkshire, B
Tel: (01535) 642

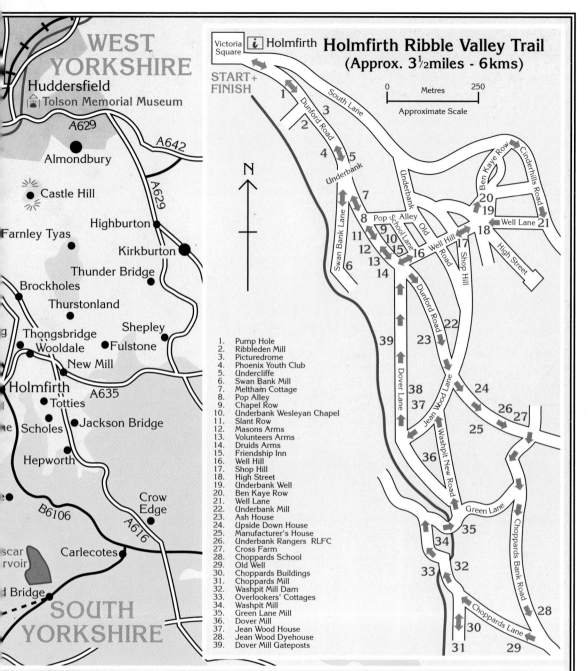

Holmfirth Ribble Valley Trail
(Approx. 3½miles - 6kms)

WEST YORKSHIRE
Huddersfield
Tolson Memorial Museum

Victoria Square   ℹ Holmfirth

START + FINISH

N

Metres   0   250
Approximate Scale

SOUTH YORKSHIRE

1. Pump Hole
2. Ribbleden Mill
3. Picturedrome
4. Phoenix Youth Club
5. Undercliffe
6. Swan Bank Mill
7. Meltham Cottage
8. Pop Alley
9. Chapel Row
10. Underbank Wesleyan Chapel
11. Slant Row
12. Masons Arms
13. Volunteers Arms
14. Druids Arms
15. Friendship Inn
16. Well Hill
17. Shop Hill
18. High Street
19. Underbank Well
20. Ben Kaye Row
21. Well Lane
22. Underbank Mill
23. Ash House
24. Upside Down House
25. Manufacturer's House
26. Underbank Rangers RLFC
27. Cross Farm
28. Choppards School
29. Old Well
30. Choppards Buildings
31. Choppards Mill
32. Washpit Mill Dam
33. Overlookers' Cottages
34. Washpit Mill
35. Green Lane Mill
36. Dover Mill
37. Jean Wood House
28. Jean Wood Dyehouse
39. Dover Mill Gateposts

Left: Edie and Glenda in deep discussion

Below: Foggy takes charge

Left: Ivy and Nora enjoying themselves

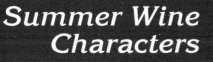

Summer Wine Characters

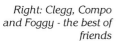

Right: Clegg, Compo and Foggy - the best of friends

Below: Compo, Seymour and Clegg at Eastergate Bridge

Below: Nora and Ivy feeling the cold

Holmfirth-Ribble Valley Trail

1. **This 4 mile (6.5 km) trail is designed to glimpse some aspects of Holmfirth's industrial archaeological past.** The starting-point on Dunford Road is the pump and trough, known as **the Pump Hole**, which in 1850 was installed by public subscription in the Underbank area to provide a water supply for surrounding houses until the late 1920s.

2. **Ribbleden Mill** provides an excellent example of many woollen mills in the area. Built in 1858 with local sandstone, its fine arched windows evoke a proud industrial past.

The Byram Arcade in Huddersfield (K)

3. **In 1850 this was an engineering workshop,** later converted into a roller-skating rink. In 1912 it became Holmfirth's first cinema, **the Picturedrome.** In the same year the **Holme Valley Theatre** was built opposite Holmfirth Parish Church, reflecting the growing popularity of motion pictures. The Picturedrome closed in 1920.

4. **The Phoenix Youth Club** rose from the ashes of the C19th National School, which fell victim to a young arsonist in 1967.

5. **Undercliffe is a splendid example of a well-to-do cloth manufacturer's house** overlooking his mill empire, which was once sited in the valley bottom. The former coach-house and stables testify to the wealth of this latter day mill-owner. Their conversion into a flat with under-garage, together with the house which is now two self-contained homes, typify a present-day trend in the utilisation of such one-time mill-owners' mansions.

6. **Site of the former Swan Bank Mill, owned by the master of Undercliffe.** Originally a woollen mill in the 1850s, it was later converted into a rug-making mill. It employed the economical technique of pegging, in which short offcuts of cloth are pushed through hessian (burlap) to form a hard-wearing patterned pile. These factory-made, pegged rag rugs were to become a popular thrifty home-based craft, though they acquired a variety of regional names, from proddy rugs or clippy rugs to stobby rugs.

7. **Meltham Cottage** exemplifies the sturdy home of a late C19th prosperous tradesman, with its solid gateposts, steps, dripstones and carved window lintels.

8. **Pop Alley,** so-called because a weary walker can 'pop up' this steep stone-setted ginnel which serves as a short-cut.

9. **Chapel Row** is a good example of a row of four terraced houses, whose occupants once shared the communal toilet at the bottom of the garden.

10. **Underbank Wesleyan Chapel** was erected in 1863 as an all-purpose building with classrooms, a kitchen, and a first-floor social room. It is large enough to have hosted theatrical events, before its closure in 1976 and its subsequent conversion into dwelling-houses and an artist's studio.

11. **Slant Row** is a group of terraced houses, so-called because their roofs follow the sloping contour of the road. Their other claim to architectural uniqueness is that they are an example of the space-saving four-storeyed 'top and bottom' houses, the top two storeys forming dwellings fronting the main road, while underneath them on Low Side are two-storeyed houses with their backs built into the ground.

12-15. These buildings are grouped together

and are evidence of the importance of the public house as a social centre for industrial communities. The newsagent's shop was formerly **the Masons Arms** (12), the last of the four pubs to close in 1951. On the opposite corner of the ginnel was **the Volunteers Arms** (13), a recruiting centre during the Boer War. Next door was **the Druids Arms** (14), and across the road was situated **the Friendship Inn** (15).

16. **Up the steep Well Hill behind the Chapel is a row of quaint cottages,** along a lane which has the confusing distinction of having a variety of names, ranging from School Lane to Low Gate to Sheep-heart Row.

The famous Castle Hill landmark (K)

17. Continuing up Well Hill, **extensive views of Holmfirth in the valley below** begin to emerge over the rooftops of descending tiers of hillside cottages. To the right is **Shop Hill,** though there are now no signs of the shop which once gave it its name.

18. Leading off a tiny square to the right is a narrow stony lane which bears the grandiose name of **High Street.** In the same area is a row of three cottages, two of which consist of a minuscule downstairs room and a bedroom over.

19. In this square is the famous **Underbank Well** from which ice-cold spring water gushes, as it is reputed to have done for the last 250 years. Most of the cottages surrounding it have been there for over 200 years, over which time their tough millstone grit exteriors have become begrimed with soot from the chimneys which characterize the Underbank skyscape. These and the narrow cobbled ginnels and snickets evoke a time which has stood still. It is little wonder that Underbank has proved an attractive location for the 'Last of the Summer Wine' film crews.

20. Left from the square is a terraced hillside lane, known as **Ben Kaye Row,** after the man who built it. Like so many lanes and houses in Underbank, it has no name plate to aid the curious visitor. Each of the terraced cottages fronting the lane is different in style, whilst artistically blending into its hillside setting.

21. Turning right up the hill, the road leads to **the separate community of Cinderhills.** Turn right down the cobbled setts of Well Lane and so back into the square, returning down Well Hill and back to Dunford Road.

22. Further up Dunford Road is the early C19th **Underbank Mill,** whose bell-tower housed the bell to summon employees to work. The firm of W. Sandford and Sons ceased business in 1978, after making cloth there since 1850.

23. Opposite is **Ash House,** another example of those imposing mill-owners' houses with a large front garden.

24. A modern upside-down house with bedrooms located beneath the living-rooms.

25. Another manufacturer's house which belonged to Underbank Mill.

26. **The playing-field of the once-renowned Underbank Rangers Rugby League Football Club,** which for nearly 100 years was the nursery for budding star players of the Huddersfield Club at Fartown. Underbank's famous son was **Harold Wagstaffe**('Waggy'), who donned the claret and gold club colours to become their captain at the age of 17, graduating to a player of national repute when he began his career with Huddersfield in 1906.

27. **Cross Farm** which has been situated at these cross-roads for nearly 200 years.

28. Going right along **Choppards Bank Road,** the countryside opens out to reveal the **River Ribble** in the valley below, with hillsides rising to **Cartworth Moor** beyond. On approaching the hamlet of Choppards is **Choppards School,** built in 1839 to double as a day school to teach children the three R's and as a Sunday School.

29. Turning right past the farm down **Choppards Lane,** there is a well on the left, once the provider of domestic water, but condemned about 60 years ago following an outbreak of typhoid fever.

30. **Choppards Buildings,** a cluster of terraced houses, is an excellent example of the home-based cloth factory. The first two storeys would serve as separate homes for families who would be employed in the large top-storey loomshop, extending over the full length of the lower storeys, and characterised by its row of weaving windows, and at the rear a once-stone staircase leading to the 'piece door' where finished pieces of cloth emerged from the workshop.

31. **The Early C19th Choppards Mill** has now been transformed into a modern house. Such mills as this were sited on the River Ribble, utilising its water-power to drive machinery and scour the cloth.

32. Returning to Choppards Lane, **Washpit Mill Dam,** is typical of all dams adjacent to mills, where a valuable water supply was stored for times when the river supply was low. Electrical power now drives any remaining mills, though water is still required for cloth processing and heating. Washpit Mill Dam serves this purpose, and provides a resource for an Angling Club.

33. **Overlookers' cottages** which housed these important mill operatives who worked round the clock.

34. Washpit Mill had small beginnings in 1810, expanding into one of the foremost mills in the region. It closed in 1980 and **textile processes now fill only part of the one remaining working mill** out of the nine which occupied Ribble Valley sites at the turn of the century. The mill gates are still closed one day each year, thus preserving a tradition which proclaims the firm's right of privacy.

35. Turning left uphill above Washpit Mill and first right down a steep lane with setted tracks to grip cartwheels, is **Green Lane Mill** built

about 1850 at the junction of Green Lane and Washpit New Road. The former location of the waterwheel can be detected in the basement next to the river bank.

36. Along Washpit New Road, the **Dover Mill** can be observed in the valley below. Originally a fulling mill in 1824, by 1905 it had become a large woollen-mill. It was destroyed by fire in 1959 and its shell has been subjected to modern development.

The busy town of Holmfirth (K)

37. Turning left down Jean Wood Lane is **Jean Wood House,** once a mill-owner's house.

38. Turning right along Dover Lane, there are the remains of the foundations of the **Jean Wood Dyehouse,** where cloth was dyed from 1828 until the waterwheel broke down in 1896.

39. Approaching the last row of houses on Dover Lane, are two stout gateposts from which were once suspended ornamental wrought-iron gates, also closed one day per year to signify the private ownership of Dover Mill. **From here is the junction with Dunford Road,** down which the Trail ends in the centre of Holmfirth.

Places to Visit & Events

Summer Wine Country extends far beyond Nora Batty's cottage and Sid's cafe. To find out more about Holmfirth and the Kirklees area as an ideal holiday centre, contact Holmfirth Tourist Information Centre.

Annual Events

HOLMFIRTH SING Just prior to Whitsuntide in Victoria Park. Singers and musicians create a concert held since 1882 to celebrate the **Holmfirth Feast**. Suited to a variety of musical tastes, it is likely to include selections from Handel's Messiah and an opportunity to hear **'Prattie Flowers', the Holmfirth anthem.**
HOLMFIRTH FOLK FESTIVAL Usually the second week in May. Begun in 1978. Events include morris, clog and longsword dancing, sing-a-rounds, and ceilidhs.
HOLME VALLEY TORCH LIGHT PROCESSION September. First held in 1078. A torch-lit procession winds its way from Thongsbridge to Holmebridge, featuring floats, brass bands, majorette groups, shire horses, and hunting packs.
HOLMFIRTH SHOPPING WEEK Begins August Bank Holiday week-end. Revival of an event dating from the 1920s. **Each year the festival adopts a different theme** which is reflected in shop-window displays, fancy dress, special organised events, and impromptu performances from street singers and dancers.

A scene from Golcar's Colne Valley Museum (K)

HONLEY SHOW Usually held on the second Saturday in June.
HONLEY CARNIVAL usually on the last Saturday in June.
HOLME VALLEY BEAGLES' COUNTRY FAIR June, at the Kennels, Upperthong. Includes falconry, farriers and ferrets!
HARDEN MOSS SHEEP DOG TRIALS Held over a week-end in mid-June at Harden Moss

on the A635 Greenfield Road. Has attracted vast crowds over many years.
PENNINE SHOW First Sunday in July at Harden Hill Farm. Attractions range from marching bands to sheepdog and beagle demonstrations.

Historic Sites and Monuments

HOLMFIRTH POSTCARD MUSEUM A collection of over 30,000 sentimental and saucy seaside postcards reflects the development of **Bamforths** over the past 100 years. A video of silent films recalls their work as pioneers in the motion picture industry, whilst another recreates the dramatic story of the Holmfirth Flood of 1852.
LAST OF THE SUMMER WINE EXHIBITION 60a Huddersfield Road, Holmfirth. The home of this fascinating exhibition is typical of the buildings which characterise both Holmfirth in reality and the **'Last of the Summer Wine'** series. Old steps lead down from the main street to a basement location, where a single room of modest size is absolutely filled with photographs and memorabilia covering 18 vintage years of filming this popular television comedy series. **The unique collection of photographs**, many never published elsewhere, is the work of **Malcolm Howarth**, a professional photographer who has built up a remarkable visual record of the programmes over the years. In that time he has formed personal friendships with many members of the cast and crew, with whom he has long been on first-name terms.There are a few small items from the series on display but the main interest of the Exhibition lies in the assembly of both black-and-white and colour photographs, which effectively map the progress of the series from the very start. Visitors who are interested in the 'Last of the Summer Wine' series should not miss the opportunity of seeing this outstanding collection of pictures - nor the chance to talk to Malcolm Howarth himself, who is a positive mine of information about the series and is also a delightful, typical Yorkshire 'character'.
CASTLE HILL off Lumb Lane, Almondbury, Huddersfield. Nearly 1,000 feet above sea level, it affords splendid panoramic views for miles around. It marks the site of early Stone Age occupation, and the magnificent ramparts of a later Bronze/Iron Age fort are clearly delineated. It evokes a vivid mental picture of life as it was when converted to a Norman motte-and-bailey settlement. It is now crowned

Last of the Summer Wine EXHIBITION

Photographs dating back to 1971

FREE ADMISSION

A superb collection of photographs
and special effects used in the
filming of the series

Exclusive Design. Summer Wine
mugs, thimbles, bells, coaster sets
and Compo's hats etc.

LAST OF THE
SUMMER WINE EXHIBITION

8 STATION ROAD,
HOLMFIRTH, HUDDERSFIELD,
WEST YORKSHIRE HD7 1AB.
TEL: (01484) 681362

by the **Jubilee Tower**, built in 1897 to celebrate the 60th anniversary of Queen Victoria's reign. Inside an exhibition traces the hill's 4,000 years of history.

TOLSON MEMORIAL MUSEUM Ravensknowle Park, Wakefield Road, Huddersfield. It displays fine collections of geology, natural history, local social history, textiles, transport, toys, glassware and silver.

COLNE VALLEY MUSEUM Cliffe Ash, Golcar, Huddersfield. Recommended by the Good Museum Guide. It is run entirely by local members and has limited opening times. The period rooms of **three restored C19th weavers' cottages** recreate a loomshop with working hand-looms and a Spinning Jenny, a weaver's living-room of 1850, and a gas-lit clogger's shop of 1910. Periodic special exhibitions and demonstrations of spinning, weaving and clog-making. Two working weekends a year are devoted to these crafts.

TUNNEL END CANAL AND COUNTRYSIDE CENTRE Reddisher Road, Marsden. Located at the entrance to Standedge Tunnel on the Huddersfield Narrow Canal, the former tunnel keeper's cottage has been restored to house a canal museum. It also interprets the surrounding Pennine countryside, and provides nature trails and canalside walks.

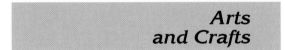

Arts and Crafts

Holmfirth has a **Craft Market** every Saturday from March to Christmas, and each July about 250 artists display their work at a major **Art and Craft Exhibition** in the Civic Hall. A wide range of craft shops sell the work of local artists, and the region's mill shops offer quality textile goods. See also the feature entitled 'Crafts and Craftsmen'.

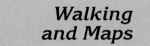

Walking and Maps

For those who wish to trace their own routes through Summer Wine Country, footpaths are clearly shown on the Ordnance Survey Pathfinder Series(1:25,000) number 714 SE 00/10 and number 702 SE 01/1l, as well as the Landranger Series(l:50,000) number 110.

TICs will have details of walks ranging from the long distance hikes to shorter strolls, such as the historic trails around Holmfirth and the surrounding area published by the Holme Valley Civic Society.

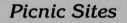

Parks

VICTORIA PARK Holmfirth. Created to celebrate the **Diamond Jubilee of Queen Victoria**, it houses the remains of the C18th Yateholme Farm which stood on the site of an ancient farmhouse recorded in the Domesday Book. It was removed to the park when a reservoir submerged the site.

BEAUMONT PARK Huddersfield. Sited on a steep, wooded hillside, there is an attractive woodland walk along an old railway branch line which ran to Meltham.

Picnic Sites

There are sites at **Digley Reservoir** near Holme, **Brownhill** and **Ramsden Rerservoirs** near Holmebridge, and **Windscar Reservoir** near Dunford Bridge. Other picnic sites are located at **Healey House** Netherton, **Golcar Appleyard, Rotcher** Slaithwaite, and **Tunnel End** Marsden. Leaflets are available to interpret the countryside surrounding some of these beauty spots.

Sports

Permits are available for **Fishing** in the area. Summer Wine Country is well supplied with **Riding Stables** and **Mountain Bikes** can be hired. There is **Sailing** on Boshaw Whams Reservoir near Hade Edge, though membership of Huddersfield Sailing Club is a requirement. Permits can be obtained for **Birdwatching** at Blackmoorfoot Reservoir near Meltham, and there are **Swimming Baths** at Holmfirth and Huddersfield. Information about all sporting activities in the area can be obtained from TICs.

Tunnel End Canal & Countryside Centre (K)

Some Crafts & Craftsmen

In this lovely rural area it comes as no surprise to find that a tradition of gardening has grown up and a number of excellent nurseries have developed in recent years to answer this need. We mention three such nurseries below, as well as one good general craft business.

TOTTIES NURSERIES are traditional growers and retailers of hardy nursery stock. This nursery was actually used for an episode of 'Last of the Summer Wine', when the three bicycle polo-players ended up under the sprinklers!

Proprietor **David Shires**, featured in the Yorkshire Post's 'Tuesday Style' column, has now established himself as one of the leading nurserymen in the county. What he has created is a plant hunter's paradise, for beginner and connoisseur alike. Any garden can easily be stocked from the thousands of varieties on offer. Plant quality and presentation are the watchwords of the nursery's success. The nursery is brimming with stock all year round, but bedding plants add an extra dash of colour at any time of season. **Hanging baskets and patio planters** are a speciality, and they too have been used on 'Last of the Summer Wine' sets.

David and his staff are always available to give helpful advice about plants and planting schemes and, with stock introduced from **'Blooms of Bressingham'**, many new and interesting varieties can now be obtained. As the nursery stands some 300 metres (nearly 1,000 feet) up in the Pennines, the plants are certainly hardy and will grow anywhere! A visit here is thoroughly recommended - even if only to enjoy the spectacular views across Summer Wine Country.

CLOUGH BOTTOM NURSERIES are another business catering to the needs of local gardeners. We should remember that by no means least among the skills that were so necessary in small rural communities was that of the gardener or cultivator of plants and vegetables. And gardening today, **'back to the soil in miniature'**, is, like so many crafts, experiencing a boom time - witness the spread of the garden centre concept - with the challenge of growing plants in different environments being eagerly met by the gardeners who throng to establishments like Clough Bottom Nurseries.

Here you will not only find all you need for your garden but you can enjoy a break in the coffee shop, where all the cakes are home made - a true taste of the South Pennines! And, of course, returning home with a few plants ensures that you will have a living souvenir of your visit to this region which will give you pleasure for years to come.

THE PENNINE GARDEN CENTRE at **Shelley near Huddersfield** is another happy hunting ground for those who want to take home a living souvenir of their visit to this beautiful area. Here will be found a wide selection of **trees and shrubs**, as well as **smaller herbaceous plants**. A particular feature is the **water garden area**, offering not only suitable plants for such an area in the garden but also a selection of pond and pool liners - and the fish to go in them.

Garden furniture is also stocked, and the staff of the Centre will always be glad to advise customers on what plants or other garden goods to select for any particular purpose. An added attraction here is the **friendly coffee shop**, open every day.

BOOTH HOUSE GALLERY, nestling in the Pennine foothills, 2½ miles (4 kms) outside Holmfirth, will surprise visitors by its spacious, beautiful showroom and the variety of high class work on show by several of the area's leading potters. The work is exhibited on two floors, adjacent to the **potters' workshop,** where visitors can see work in progress at weekends.

Gallery owner **Jim Robison** is a nationally known potter, whose own work is in collections world wide and who has collaborated with many architects around Britain to produce ceramic murals to decorate buildings such as hospitals, shopping centres and offices.

There is a remarkable variety of work on show, so whatever your taste or the state of your finances you will almost certainly find something to buy at Booth House Gallery to remind you of your visit to Holmfirth.

Many people like to have a memento of a **special occasion** such as a christening, wedding or anniversary, and Jim will gladly accept **commissions** to make a special, inscribed pot, mug or plate for such an occasion. The result is a gift which is truly unique. Many visitors return again and again, and Booth House Gallery welcomes all customers, both old and new.

Summer Wine Villages

The River Holme rises just below Holme Moss and meanders north for about 8 miles (13 kms) to join the River Colne at Huddersfield. Above its course, hillside villages encapsulate within modern development the fascinating history of Summer Wine Country. They also provide a myriad of locations for the 'Last of the Summer Wine' TV series.

BROCKHOLES This is an excellent centre from which to walk through enchanting woodland - **ideal badger country**, reflected in the name of the village. Its houses are clustered among a huge outcrop of rock which appropriately gives its name to the village inn, The Rock.

COOK'S STUDY Not a village, but an area of moorland, high above Holmfirth to the south, where our story of Holme Valley man began. The discovery of flints is evidence that about 4,000 years ago the **first Stone Age settlement** in Summer Wine Country was at Cook's Study. There was a 5 metre (16 foot) high wooden tower here in the C18th, purportedly erected as an observatory by a vicar interested in astronomy. It became known as 'Cook's Study', but was destroyed between 1798 and 1814 during disturbances following the passing of a local Enclosure Act. Another tower soon occupied the same site. A famous C19th sculptor, **Sir Francis Chantry**, was so impressed with the view over Summer Wine Country that he drew up plans for a tower from which to contemplate the scene in comfort. Unfortunately, he died before his idea was carried out. However, **Sir John Spencer Stanhope**, utilised his friend's plan to build a stone monument to his memory in 1852. The 12 metre (40 foot) high tower was inscribed Chantry Tower, though the name of the first tower, 'Cook's Study', lingered on. People from miles around journeyed to enjoy the panoramic views and take a drink at the nearby Cart and Horses pub, now no longer in existence. Badly damaged by fire in 1860, the tower was still used as a gamekeeper's house and shooting-lodge until about 1890. Then it began to disintegrate, until it was demolished in 1934 to make way for quarrying. Cook's Study may have disappeared, but the views over the Holme Valley which broaden out over the whole panorama of Kirklees, still remain. **Cook's Study is a vantage point** from which visitors can open the curtains on Summer Wine Country, contemplate its long history, and close the curtains before returning home.

HADE EDGE Set amidst windswept hilltop moorland south of Holmfirth, the houses and occupants of Hade Edge brace themselves against exposure to the elements. Below it to the south-west, a delightful valley opens up, with **Holme Styes Reservoir** fringed in pine trees providing a delightful centrepiece. This is a place of wild solitude where the wanderer amongst the derelict farmsteads of Hades, Elysium and Copthurst, can savour the harsh life of its former farmers, weavers, and quarrymen. The wildness of the countryside apparently infected its former occupants, as many stories testify. It was here that the men of Hades were locked out of the chapel during a rush-bearing service because of their drunken behaviour. In 1850 a Hade Edge man was brought before the courts for hiring out a cock-pit in breach of God's Sabbath Law. In his defence he claimed that God could know nothing of Hade Edge as it was too far out! He was fined five shillings! Today's villagers fill their leisure hours with less disreputable pursuits, many of them involved with the highly successful **Hade Edge Brass Band**.

The beautiful setting of Scammonden Reservoir (K)

HEPWORTH This is an Anglo-Saxon settlement, aptly named from 'hep' meaning 'high' and 'worth' a 'dwelling'. Farming and handloom-weaving were responsible for its early expansion, and in the C19th coal-mining and Dobroyd's textile mill promoted further growth. By 1664 Hepworth had developed into a township, and became an independent parish around the **Church of the Holy Trinity**, often used for 'Last Of The Summer Wine' location shots. Its population was depleted in 1665 by the London Plague, thought to have been imported in clothing sent to Foster Place. The spread of infection was halted by the prompt action of building a barricade, now known as **Barracks Fold**. In the C17th, Hepworth became the first Summer Wine village to establish a free school, and the present school was an early Board School set up in the 1880s. **Hepworth Feast,** held on the last Monday in June, possibly has pagan origins related to Midsummer's Eve, though tradition conveniently linked it to deliverance from the Plague of 1665.

The forbidding Pennine Hills (K)

HOLME At 274 metres (900 feet) above sea level, this is the valley's uppermost village. Though one of the oldest settlements of Holme Valley man, its present day fame rests with the **Holme Moss TV mast** which pierces the skyline to the south. Erected in the early 1950s and periodically open to the public, this 221 metre (725 foot) high transmitter was the first to serve the north of England. Another of Holme's modern features is **'Underhill'**, the unusual house of the architect **Arthur Quarmby** which is built underground and has a lawn for its roof! Its older buildings bear witness to a thriving past. The 1838 date stone on the Sunday School belies the true age of the building, as evidenced by an inscription of 1694 on a lower lintel. Another engraved stone identifies **'Holme Board School, 1880'**. The southernmost houses, just before the bridge over Rake Dyke, are an example of early sheep-farming homesteads. The lower one marks the site of the former Peacock Inn where the **Ancient Order of Shepherds** held their first meeting in 1830. Along Fieldhouse Lane leading to Meltham, the early textile industry is recalled in pairs of holes in the wall to which tenter hooks were affixed to hold drying yarn. The significant role that wool once played in the life of Holme is perpetuated in the name of the village pub, **'The Fleece'**, a longtime venue for meets of foxhounds and beagles. This picturesque village provides an excellent starting point for moorland, woodland and reservoir walks, all of which afford extensive panoramic views over Summer Wine Country.

HOLMFIRTH See separate feature.

HONLEY Next to Holmfirth, Honley is the largest village in Summer Wine Country. Modern housing dominates its outer edges, but its centre still provides evidence of a vigorous historical past. In Church Street a building designated 'Exchange', and dated 1751, was once the **'Wool Exchange'** where wool was bought by domestic weavers. Many of their cottages can be found grouped around enclosed 'yards', as they are known in Holmfirth, though called 'folds' in Honley. Sitting in the bar of The Coach and Horses, the visitor can recall that it was here in 1812 that **Benjamin Walker and Thomas Smith, two members of a Luddite gang** of four, spent the night carousing, having murdered a Marsden mill-owner, William Horsfall. Later all four were brought to trial in York and the landlady of The Coach and Horses, Mrs Robinson, was called to give evidence. A further reminder of Honley's more turbulent past are the village stocks, sited by **St. Mary's Church** gates, next to a font, originally in Honley Chapel before the church was built in 1843. At the bottom of Church Street are the **Town Wells** erected in 1796, and to the right is the old pinfold where stray cattle were impounded until claimed by their owners. These are only a few of the intriguing landmarks which characterise Honley. Visitors will be rewarded by further delights by wandering within its confines.

NEW MILL This village is an offspring of the ancient hamlet of **Fulstone** which lies to its north-east. The site of the manorial mill, from which New Mill took its name, is now under the mill at Glendale, where the first Holme Valley scribbling engine was erected in 1780. By the early C19th, New Mill was a thriving township. The Halifax to London coach, the 'Hope', stopped twice a day at the Duke of Leeds, then one of four town inns of which only The White Hart still survives. Entering New Mill from Holmfirth, the gracious lines of **Lydgate Chapel**, built in 1768 and remodelled in 1848, conceal its long history as a Presbyterian foundation of 1695, though Unitarian since the C18th. Another building worthy of note is the old brewery now converted to private dwellings. Above its archway were once etched the words **'New Mill Brewery'**, though today only 'Brewery' remains, as 'New Mill' was obliterated during the Second World War to conceal geographical information from possible invading German forces. New Mill, with its satellite old clothiers' hamlets and relics of mine workings, is a paradise for industrial archaeologists. Ascending Sudehill towards the 1831 parish church, yards and ginnels remain untouched by time. Off to the right is **Jubbs Road**, a memorial to a family of millwrights and machine-makers. Behind the old 1838 National School, is **Barraclough Row**, which dates back to 1841 when all the houses were occupied by families named Barraclough. Above New Mill, along Hirst Lane to the south-east, is **'Mount'**, once a busy hilltop community. From here can be viewed hillsides riddled with abandoned coal workings. Amongst them, two pits, Sally Wood and Woodpit, survived until 1947. **Gin Pit Lane** recalls a pit powered by a gin-engine, driven by a pony going round in circles. To the south is Meal Hill, the country home of small-time coal owner **Uriah Tinker** and his family for over 200 years. Their name lives on in Tinker's Tower and Tinker's Hill, a panoramic setting east of **Jackson Bridge** which is used extensively in the 'Last Of The Summer Wine' series. Near **Meltham House** was the entrance to a tramway tunnel which once connected Bank House Pit with the Crowedge Iron End Clay workings. Its route can still be traced, and walls and gates, incorporating old tramway rails, serve as reminders of the tunnel's former life. The countryside around New Mill, with its geological mix of sandstone, coal, shale and clay, is one of the softer and more fertile areas of Summer Wine Country.

SCHOLES Once a Viking settlement, it became distinguished as **a village constructed entirely of millstone grit**, whereas other villages originally contained many sandstone structures. Its lofty position affords glorious views to the east, whilst one of its districts, Paris (pronounced Pairis), is particularly photogenic. The 'Boot and Shoe Inn' was an early C19th coaching house, and today no doubt its local patrons will proudly remind the visitor that Scholes is the **birthplace of Roy Castle**, the popular entertainer and devotee of the area's brass band tradition.

TOTTIES The main claim to fame of this tiny hamlet is Totties Hall, a small manor house built on a large estate in 1684 by Henry Jackson, one-time Quaker dissenter who was imprisoned for his beliefs. His name lives on in the picturesque village of JACKSON BRIDGE which houses the White Horse Inn, featured as the 'local' in the 'Last Of The Summer Wine' series. Henry Jackson constructed the bridge over New Mill Dyke to shorten his journeys between his old house at Meal Hill and his more sumptuous residence at Totties.

UPPERTHONG AND NETHERTHONG When viewed from the ancient cottages on Wolfstone Heights over Wolfstone Hall below, it is easy to deduce how its Domesday Book name is derived from 'Thoac' a 'tongue of land'. Perched on a hilltop to the west of Holmfirth, one of Upperthong's attractions is the lychgate of the **Church of St John the Evangelist**, consecrated in 1848. In a fold to the left of the main street, **Towngate**, is the old manor house which has been divided into four cottages. Having made a stop-over at The Royal Oak with its collection of antiques, a journey over **Wolfstone Heights** will bring the visitor to **Netherthong.** A circle of old cottages forms this charming hilltop village, and the 'Last Of The Summer Wine' series has put its photogenic qualities to good use. It possesses two places of worship, the **Methodist Chapel**, known locally as 'T'Zion', and the **Wesleyan Chapel** on the Thongsbridge Road which was visited by John Wesley in 1772.

The pretty setting of Digley Reservoir (K)

WOOLDALE Referred to as **'Vluedal'** in the Domesday Book, this neighbouring village to Totties was also greatly influenced by the Jackson family. At the bottom of Pell Lane, **Henry Jackson** founded the **Meeting House of the Society of Friends**, visited in 1669 by **George Fox**, founder of the Quaker movement. Jackson's eldest son, Elihu, built Wooldale Hall which stands next to the Wesleyan Chapel. The Lord Nelson pub had a predecessor in The Bay Horse, opened in 1691, now a private house standing in **Pell Lane.** In its gable end are the holes of a very unusual dovecote. The centre of the village bears the hallmarks of the textile industry, especially the high dwellings of former handloom weavers in **South Street**. From here, **Luddites** plotted the destruction of the new machinery. Amongst ancient cottages, stands one at the bottom of South Street which still retains an external stone staircase leading to the 'piece-door' or 'taking-in' door in its gable end.

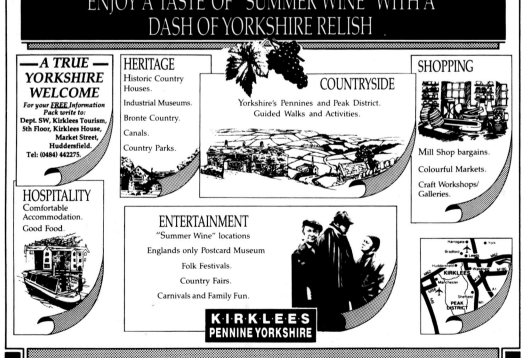